God Guides Your Tomorrows

HOW TO BE CONFIDENT THAT GOD IS LEADING YOUR LIFE

Roger C. Palms

INTERVARSITY PRESS
DOWNERS GROVE, ILLINOIS 60515

Revised edition ©1987 by Roger C. Palms

First edition ©1976 by Augsburg Publishing House.

Originally published under the title God Holds Your Tomorrows.

*InterVarsity Press is the book-publishing division of InterVarsity Christian
Fellowship, a student movement active on campus at hundreds of universities,
colleges and schools of nursing. For information about local and regional
activities, write Public Relations Dept., InterVarsity Christian Fellowship, 6400
Schroeder Rd., P.O. Box 7895, Madison, WI 53707-7895.*

*Distributed in Canada through InterVarsity Press, 860 Denison St., Unit 3,
Markham, Ontario L3R 4H1, Canada.*

*All Scripture quotations, unless otherwise indicated, are from the Holy Bible,
New International Version. Copyright © 1973, 1978, International Bible
Society. Used by permission of Zondervan Bible Publishers.*

Cover photograph: Robert Cushman Hayes

ISBN 0-87784-572-7

Printed in the United States of America

Library of Congress Cataloging in Publication Data

Palms, Roger C.
  God guides your tomorrows.

  *Previous ed. published as: God holds your
tomorrows.   1976.*
    1. God—Will.   2. Christian life—1960-
I. Title.
BV4501.2.P319   1986   248.4   86-27688
ISBN 0-87784-572-7

*This special edition is published with permission from the original
publisher, InterVarsity Press.*

Preface

The question keeps coming up.

Probably because it's too important to ignore. Get a group of serious Christians together and someone will ask: "How can I know the will of God for my life?"

For years—first as a pastor ministering to students at Rutgers and Douglass, then as a campus minister at Michigan State University, and now as a magazine editor and teacher—I've been asked that same question. It isn't a light question. It comes out of an honest yearning to know. Those years of walking on campus late at night with a searching student, of talking with questioning high-school students, of counseling adults, of listening to the struggling, the hurting, the sensitive wonderer, have led to the writing of this book. And, as I've worked on this manuscript, people have commented on the need for it, encouraging me as I went along.

"How can I know the will of God for my life?" is too critical a question to go unanswered. Thousands of Christians really want to know, "Does God hold my tomorrows?"

You may be one of those who are asking.

You're the reason for this book.

1

A Reason
for Me

As *far as I'm concerned, when God made me he* made a big mistake."

She was sitting on the floor when she said it, the fireplace casting the only light over the seven other people in the room. They couldn't see her well, but they could see the tears glistening.

Two attempts at suicide underscored what she was saying—still, no one responded to her. Later, four of the others said that they couldn't respond because they were feeling the same way about themselves. So do some of us.

Is there a reason for me? In the whole scope of the world, with life as confusing as it is, what did God have in mind when he made me? As a matter of fact, I wonder if God had anything in mind at all.

In this confusing conglomeration of ideas and dreams, weaknesses and moods called life, is there anything of value about me or for me?

Something happens to me when I ask those questions. There comes a feeling, an awe, an awareness. I am asking about me, and the only one who can answer my questions shows me by my very asking that he has, or is himself, the answer. If God is God, with no limits to his knowledge or understanding, then there is a reason for me and he knows what it is.

Don't Argue with God

God's omnipotence didn't collapse when I was conceived. His mouth didn't drop open in surprise the day I was born. In the whole arrangement of things, I fit. If there is a question left at all, it is not, "Do I belong here?" It is rather, "How do I belong?"

God knows who I am, what I am and why he put me here. I am no accident. Sometimes, though, it is tough to grasp. At least it is until I lean back for a moment, shut my eyes and reflect.

No one was around to argue or disagree when God created the first man and woman. No one heard his pronouncement about them. God repeated it for the writer of Genesis because he wanted us to know. What he said about us, his creation, is not an observation to argue. It is a statement of fact. God looked at the ones he made, the crowning of his creation, and pronounced them "good." He must have meant what he said.

Yet some of us want to argue with him now.

A man looks at his racquetball partner and wishes he

could have the same physique.

A woman screams at God because she is lonely, then becomes silent, withdrawn.

A school dropout takes two more tranquilizers and mutters about his lack of opportunity. Two old men open a bottle and talk about what might have been.

Yet, the Word of God still stands: God likes what he made. "That's good," he said when he made the first man and woman, and there is no evidence in all the centuries since that he has ever changed his mind—even when he made each of us.

Getting You Here

Think for a minute about all that God did to get you here. In the universal plan of God, with all the people in the world whom he might have created, he specifically, purposely, knowingly, brought together our great-grandparents and grandparents and parents to put together the selected combination of talents, features and mental gifts to make us what we are.

We are not mistakes.

But wait. Is this also true for the person whose parents didn't want him, for the one who is the product of a mistake or a crime? Did God know? Did he plan it?

God alone can answer the mystery of his own knowledge. He alone knows how to bring good out of what to human minds seems catastrophic. And we know that he does.

Our questions about how God can know and plan good from something we call evil aren't usually balanced by the opposite questions—but they should be: How can it be that God can bring together committed

Christians to produce a bright and attractive child, to love that child and raise him in the nurture and admonition of the Lord, only to see him throw it all over, to reject it all for the wretchedness of an existence apart from God? But it happens. Ideal examples of the "plan of God" crumble just as often as examples of poor possibilities become God's trophies of blessing and grace.

The only conclusion is, God never meets the unexpected, God knows and God loves. When these affirmations come together in our minds, we can turn back to the assurance that "there are no surprises with God." No one of us is an exception to that. In God's own moment of time he put us here, a perfect combination of all that he intended us to be.

What would your life have been if you had lived five hundred years ago in Mongolia, or even today in regions of the Sahara? Ask yourself what divine intervention made you what you are and put you where you are now—in this place at this time. The "chance" factor is staggering. What God has done, God has done. What he has allowed, he has allowed. What he will do, he will do. His will is both creative and permissive. God knows what he is doing!

He Is Not Confused by Us
I'm unique. You are too. I'm here now, in this time and place, and you are where you are, and God is not confused by our presence.

When that thought begins to dawn on people, the results are interesting to watch. Slowly, like a flower in the sunshine, people begin to unfold. They take another look.

Joni Eareckson Tada became a paraplegic when she was a teen-ager. Since then she has become an artist and singer with a ministry called "Joni and Friends." She was absolutely right when she told a group of journalists, "With God, less is more."

A schoolteacher in England cannot use his hands. He is also blind. His crippling illness came just as he was preparing for college studies. But through his suffering, he came to recognize that God is God. He came to a trusting faith and says, after years of suffering and struggle, that he is a contented teacher, pleased that he can help others and support himself. "The day I paid my first taxes was a very happy day for me."

A young widow, deciding that God knew what was happening when she was left to support two little girls, trained herself as a writer so she wouldn't have to leave home to work. Today she is still being regularly published—in her eighties.

This Package Called *Me* Is Free

For nearly all of us the awareness that God is God and has a reason for our existence and has put together the package that is called me and likes what he made and wants to develop and fulfill what he has made as a unique and special individual, has led us to something deeper than personal, social or vocational changes—it has led to a totally new life.

For centuries, Christian believers have known what some of us are only beginning to discover: that the biblical word *salvation* means freedom. Salvation is a picture word—it is like breaking out of a box or cell and running free on the beach. It is liberation that touches and transforms every dimension of our being.

It is life as God meant it to be.

Still, the majority of people in the world don't yet know that. Sadly, they are like square pegs in round holes.

They are created by God, but they don't know God. They live in a world that he made, but are out of harmony with him as their maker. They function as best they can by the natural laws established by a teacher who understands all things, without knowing the teacher. They have many of the expressions of God's love, but not God the source.

But it is not that way for those of us who respond to the liberator—Jesus Christ. In him we find a new relationship centered in all that God is. We meet the source, the teacher, the creator—God!

Liberated persons know that God has made them exactly the way he wants them—in a manner that is pleasing to him—then offers wholeness and fulfillment through the saving work of Jesus Christ.

Alive to Begin

People like to say, "I'm saved! Praise God! The old has gone, the new has come!" And that's true. But it's true in the same way that birth is new. When anyone is at last alive in Christ Jesus, he is alive to begin. He doesn't work for his salvation. That's a gift. But he does work out the implications of his salvation "with fear and trembling" (Phil 2:12).

That's a long process—it never ends. Day by day we bring more and more of our lives under the searching gaze of Christ. The purity, the compassion, the indwelling power of God pokes and prods farther and farther into our lives showing us day after day additional aspects of ourselves that need to be cleansed and made new. And we see, because God makes us see, that there is still more of ourselves to yield to him.

That's part of maturing in Christ. We are both complete and growing. We are his, yet are always becoming more like him as we come into his fullness. We take from the fullness of the one who wants to be in all that we are now and all that we are yet to be.

In the new birth the vise grip of sin that once had us bound tight, that kept us separated from God, is broken. All of the uncertainties ("Where did I come from?" "Why am I here?" "Where am I going?") are ready for a new evaluation. We're free to develop, free to be in harmony with the one who created us, saved us and loves us.

That's almost too much to comprehend.

A Very Intimate Word
This relationship is so different from anything else we know, and such a change from what we once were, that the only explanation of it is the biblical one—it is a moving out of darkness into light. Attempting to explain this, St. Paul used an Aramaic word that can't quite be translated, but it does communicate a feeling. To everyone who through the atoning work of Jesus Christ moves out of the place of tension and antagonism into a place of harmony with God, there is given the privilege of calling God *Abba*. It means "Father."

Only *Abba* is a more intimate word for Father. The closest the English language comes is a reverent "my daddy."

Some people, offended at this translation, argue that such a word is sacrilegious. And, if it is used without the proper awe of God, it is. But to anyone who worships God, it is a descriptive term that means love, security and peace. To those who understand, the cry *Abba* is like coming home.

Debbie was nineteen when she came home. She did trust Jesus as her Savior, but even so she was bringing with her an uneasy lifetime of unhappy experiences with men. And it was hard for her to forget.

She felt dirty inside. She struggled with guilt. She knew that she had been cleansed and was pure in Christ, yet she still felt that she could not live the new life that she had just received. She could not hold up her head and proclaim, "I'm a Christian." There were too many scars on her soul.

No one had yet explained to her what spiritual adoption means. Then one day a new friend, a Christian, did.

Very tenderly he asked, "Debbie, if God is your father and he is my father, what does that make you and me?"

She knew, of course. "That makes us brother and sister." It was a small step but already a new awareness was coming over this much-experienced young woman. Her new brother didn't stop there.

"Now let me show you something else. If God is your father and he is Lord and King, what does that make you?"

She thought for a minute and then a smile slowly pushed against the edges of her mouth. "I guess that would make me the King's daughter—I'm a princess!"

"Exactly! Now go live what you are."

And she is.

A Price Tag

Jeff came from a different direction but still he was a lot like Debbie. He didn't know what he was worth. From childhood he had been reminded of his failures. He had come to believe that he was a failure. Even becoming a Christian hadn't done much to alter his inferiority complex. He still tended to keep to the edges, away from other people, and hold onto his conviction that he wasn't as capable as others—not in doing, not in thinking, not even in loving. Because he believed this, it kept him bound up, unable to try the life that God had given him.

Then through careful study of the Scriptures and listening to Christians around him, he gained a new insight. Slowly, what he has been learning is altering his attitude about himself. He is starting to reach out and people are responding to him.

What made the difference? He has an explanation, something he learned. "I have a price tag on me, just like anything else that is up for redemption. And that price tag says, 'Jesus Christ.' "

"Do you want to know what I'm worth to God the Father? I'm worth the price he paid for me—I'm worth Jesus. If you can tell me the worth of Jesus, I'll tell you what I am worth, because Jesus is the price God paid for me." And with a contented smile Jeff adds, "And God knew what he was buying!"

A Man Called Happy

Some people scoff at Jeff's simplicity, but most don't. They've been wondering about their worth too. Finding out how much God loves us is like going through a doorway. It opens out to a whole new world.

A few years ago in a rescue mission in the Midwest, a man called Happy sat on an organ bench and began to play. It was early. People from the streets hadn't started to drift in yet. But that was just as well, because he had a story to tell.

"I was fifty-nine years old and tired. I didn't want to play the organ anymore. I felt weary and restless at the same time. A lot of years had gone by since I became a professional. In those days I thought that what I really wanted out of life was fame and the chance to earn a lot of money.

"Well, I was earning the money, but I didn't want it! I just wanted to quit. I was sick of performing, bored with my music and disgusted with my own jokes.

"So I asked the casino manager in Nevada, where I was playing the organ, if I could cancel my last week. He said, 'No, stay on. You're drawing the crowds.'

"I finished that week, did a two-week stint at a small supper club in Twin Falls, Idaho, simply as a favor to a friend, and then moved on to Spokane, Washington. When I got there, I took a room and did nothing.

"I knew something was happening in my life, but I couldn't put my finger on it. All I knew for sure was that the things I once wanted didn't satisfy me anymore. I had a talent for music and a miserable life.

"One Saturday I went to see a Christian businessman I knew in the city and blurted out what for me was a strange plea: 'I need prayer.'

"As far as I can remember it was the first time that I had ever asked anyone to pray for me.

"We got down on our knees in the basement of his

store and prayed. I was crying my heart out because I needed God in my life and I knew it. A lot was settled in that basement that day. I knew I was a new creation."

Coming to the Lord was like moving into the stream of God's purposes. For Happy, everything that he had, including his gift for playing the organ, came into focus. The anxiety was gone.

"The next afternoon, I went to see the superintendent of the Gospel mission and asked him if he would like to have me play at the services.

"He said, 'We'd love to have you.'

"That was Sunday. The following Wednesday, as I was on my way out of the hotel, I got a telephone call from a club manager asking me to do a Gay Nineties' routine at a new place he was opening. I knew I could do it. I'm big. I look like a bartender. But I told him I was going to play at the mission. He congratulated me. That surprised me. Here was a man who wanted me to play for him and he was congratulating me for refusing his offer.

"I'm in my seventies now, and I've been playing in missions around the country for more than thirteen years. When I was younger, I always looked down on missions. I thought the people there were just a bunch of winos. I didn't have any compassion. I just assumed that it was their hard luck.

"But now I like to go over to the mission about a half hour before the evening meeting begins and play as the people come in. I notice that when I'm playing a quietness comes over them and they respond to it. It softens them. They like to hear me play. That pleases me."

It's a new world when we discover who we are, why

we have been made, and why we were put here on this earth. Some of us find it out early, others—like Happy—find it late. But what matters is that we do find it and begin to experience life in its multidimensional fullness—satisfying and abundant.

Each of us can then declare with certainty:

"I'm no accident."

"I fit into God's plan."

"I belong."

"God has a reason for me."

There is relief and there is purpose in discovering that. Most of all there is peace. It is a peace that comes from knowing with unswerving certainty, "I have been created for a reason. I am offered a life to live by the One who understands the reason for my being."

No One Else Has My Fingerprints

In the whole pattern of the universe, God made only one person like me. Just as no one else has my fingerprints, so no one else can be the person I am. God designed me to be special.

So much unnecessary struggle continues when we refuse God and refuse to fit into life as God meant it to be. When we could be whole, we remain fragmented. When we could know the will of God for our lives, some of us won't even acknowledge that there is a will of God.

Those who hold back, who still refuse to transfer their trust from themselves to the Son of God, still wonder in the thoughtful moments of their lives—"Why me?"

But for those who look to him, yield and find their true selves, the fears of now and the future start to go. The uncertainties about personal worth give way to the exhilarating, "Look who I am."

When that happens, the reason for living becomes what the apostle Paul called "Christ in you, the hope of glory" (Col 1:27). Then at last the words of Jesus make sense: "I came that they may have life, and have it abundantly" (Jn 10:10 RSV).

Aimless drifting changes to purpose. Questions that once tore us apart at last start to get answered. Life's pieces start to fit together and the once confusing mix called existence begins to jell. The content of Psalm 139 makes sense. The prospects for each of us become unlimited and exciting.

It is no longer, "Why am I here?" but, "I am here and I am his."

2

What Does God Want from Me Anyway?

They *meant well.*

Before Ron and Judy were married, they talked about serving Christ in the inner city. They wanted to work among the poor, teach Bible classes to children and help adults find new dignity in Christ.

But now, eighteen years later in a grassy suburb, they are so locked into mortgage payments, credit purchases and the need to keep comfortable employee fringe benefits that they can't move. Ron says, "I'm three weeks from bankruptcy. I can't even afford to get sick. I'm so overextended that when I go to bed at night I lie awake with money pressures on my mind." Then he adds, "The worst part of it is, we are no longer available." Once, with a promise to obey, they both asked, "What does

God want to do with me?" Neither one of them asks that question anymore. They are owned.

Lenny is twenty years old. He is owned by heroin. He calls it "my medicine."

Christians have talked with him about following Jesus but it doesn't do any good. He says, "I am following Jesus." He thinks he's all right—it's the other Christians who don't understand, he says. "I'm high-strung, my nerves are bad—this is my medication." Then he rationalizes, "Nobody gets upset with a diabetic who takes insulin. No one tells him to stop taking it. Why am I so different? Why can't God use me the way I am? What does God want from me anyway?"

Well, what does God want? If I am a disciple, a follower of Jesus, then in one clear statement Jesus gives me the answer to my question. He says, "Blessed rather are those who hear the word of God and obey it" (Lk 11:28).

God Wants Obedience

It's my business to find out what God wants of me and then do what he says. God wants obedience—not success, not prestige or power, not anything but obedience. Read the "Hall of Fame" list in Hebrews 11. It is a roster of obedient people.

But most of us tend to become a little soft on obedience. We leak out at the edges. We follow Christ in intermittent spurts. And soon it is with a tinge of annoyance that we demand: "What does God want from me anyway?"

What God wants isn't based so much on doing, although that's the measurable part of obedience. It's being. God wants me to be what he created me to be, and to be in the place where he can lead me. Being in Christ means having him in us—doing, acting, working through us—so that even though we can only measure the doing, it is built on the being. Like Enoch of old our contribution to life and the world around us comes not from ourselves—it comes, when all is said and done, because we "walked with God" (Gen 5:24).

To be is to live—and living in Christ means being in Christ. Like the vine and the branches, being means to be so closely attached that the life-giving energy of the vine flows through the branches and the branches bear fruit (see Jn 15:4). Abiding means "having the eyes of your hearts enlightened." It means knowing "the hope to which he has called you," having "the riches of his glorious inheritance in the saints," and "the immeasurable greatness of his power in us" (Eph 1:18-19 RSV).

Abiding is natural for people alive in Christ. "If anyone is in Christ he is a new creation" (2 Cor 5:17). And, how do we measure that or test it? The Bible says, "By their fruit you will recognize them" (Mt 7:16). God will be in us as we abide in him. The result is the fruit of that abiding: "love, joy, peace, patience, kindness, goodness, faithfulness, gentleness and self-control" (Gal 5:22-23). The question is not, will he give all of that to me? The question is, will I abide? It isn't weakness to admit that on my own I can't abide in him. Only his new nature in me makes that possible. He helps me. An abiding Christian knows that.

Are the Fences Too High?

Maturity in Christ means agreeing with God that I am

a straying sheep who needs controls. It's an understanding. It is a confession that I know myself. Most of all
it is an admission that God knows me too. After thirty
years of obedience, the apostle Paul still knew that
struggle. He said, "I do not understand what I do. For
what I want to do I do not do, but what I hate I do. And
if I do what I do not want to do, I agree that the law
is good. As it is, it is no longer I myself who do it, but
it is sin living in me" (Rom 7:15-17).

For all of us, that struggle will go on as long as we
live. It is a tension, but just as tension is effective in
body building, so it is in spirit building. God gave us
laws to obey. They are guides, built on the structure of
his own great love. To be his follower is to be obedient
to him and live within the boundaries of his laws.

But for some, the legal boundaries of God's love look
like fences, and they seem to be too high. When I want
God but not his commands, I may ask, "What does God
want from me?" But he knows—and I know too—
whether I really want to find out. He knows whether I
am just saying words or if I do want to be a disciple.
Some people say it, but they don't mean it.

On the East Coast a young woman asked her pastor,
"Why can't I find the will of God for my life?" The pastor
can't help her, though he tries. The reason he can't is
that she rejects every suggestion he makes. In fact, she
is living two lives. Most of the year she is active in her
church, teaches Sunday school, and quotes Scripture at
appropriate times. But during her summer vacations she
flies to the West Coast and spends three weeks living on
the beaches, spending her nights with any man she can
find. "I can't help it," she says. "I'm oversexed. That's

the way God made me." Then she goes right back to asking her original question, "Why can't I find the will of God for my life?"

To ask about the will of God is easy—to want to obey the will of God is something else. God does have a direction for us to go. He does want us to belong to the pattern of life that will complete and satisfy us—but he will not move if we are pushing against him. James explained it well. "God opposes the proud but gives grace to the humble" (Jas 4:6). Some of us are standing in opposition to God, and he is harder than a stone wall. The grace of God, which crosses all barriers, is lost to us. Two students caught this in a short dialog:

"God promised abundant life if I seek it. He isn't going to keep me from it. If I don't get it, it's because I don't ask."

"Maybe, but some don't get it because God knows they aren't going to live it. Much of the problem with learning the will of God is in myself. Can God trust me with his revealed will—will I follow him?"

Once God sees that I do want to follow him and obey him, and that I will abide in him, then I can be sure that he will lead me. When he sees that I am prayerfully searching for and obeying whatever truth he reveals in small parts, he will continue to reveal that much more of himself to me.

God Can Open the Windows

God didn't promise help for just pieces of our lives. " 'Test me in this,' says the LORD Almighty, 'and see if I will not throw open the floodgates of heaven and pour out so much blessing that you will not have room enough for it' " (Mal 3:10). He said that about life itself. Go ahead, try him! Look what God can do in just one area—choosing a vocation. Ask around and you will meet people who can thrill you with stories about what God has done in this and other areas of their lives.

Many times I've watched as God has put together a combination of experiences and education to shape a person for a position that didn't even exist while they were being prepared. Then when their training was completed, the job appeared. We may be limited in our planning by what is now—but God is not. He wants to lead. He knows what is ahead—he knows each of us.

Hundreds of clergyman today owe their knowledge of Greek and the interpretation of the New Testament to a Christian scholar who as a student got into the wrong registration line. He thought it was the registration for a Latin class. When he got to the desk, he found he was in the line for Greek. But, being comfortable in the leading of God, he stayed in line and enrolled in the Greek course. God was in that move. He went on to become a New Testament Greek scholar who influenced thousands in the Christian church.

God wants us ready. It doesn't matter how impossible something seems. When we are ready, he will lead us through ways that seem impossible. And as he leads, he is very economical. Even the odd things we are doing now will be just the background we need someday for the next step in his leading. When we are in his will, he doesn't waste anything. There is real peace in knowing that. When God is in control, nothing is too difficult.

Those Special Arrangements

When I felt a strong call to the ministry, I enrolled for fall quarter at a seminary even though I didn't have the money or my college diploma. Before my final college quarter began, I learned that I needed four specific courses to complete my major and earn my degree. But could I get the right two courses spring quarter and the remaining two in summer school?

That was one obstacle. The other was that I also had to work full time to earn enough money to enter seminary.

I couldn't figure it out, but I could pray. So when it came time to register for classes spring quarter, I prayed and blindly chose two of the four courses I needed in my major field. I still did not know what would be offered that summer. There was no way I could anticipate and balance my spring-quarter schedule with the summer schedule. I registered and waited.

A few weeks later the summer schedule was posted, offering only two courses in my major—the exact two that I needed to graduate. And they were offered on alternate evenings at 7 P.M.—so I could work days if I could get a job.

It wasn't long before my part-time employer asked if I would be able to work full time that summer on a special job that had just been set up for that summer only. He didn't stop there. Would I be willing to start an hour earlier each day, then quit at 4 P.M. instead of 5 P.M.?

So I got my classes, got my full-time job, and God even gave me the bonus of extra time to eat supper and study before class each night.

There are no halfway steps with God.

Faithfulness Doesn't Always Buy Success

God does not fail his people. He never has and he never will. That doesn't mean that I might not suffer in his will, or even die for my obedience. But as one person put it after a little reflection, "So what?"

Faithfulness doesn't always bring success or victory. It didn't for the apostle John. He was exiled.

It didn't for Paul. He went to prison.

It didn't for John the Baptist. He did what God called him to do and had his head served up on a platter.

It didn't for Stephen. He was martyred by stoning.

The will of God is exactly that—the will of God. It is not my will. I am not called to be successful but to be his. I may not have great results in my life, but I am called to be faithful.

Believers have lost their homes and incomes taking a stand for what is right. Christians have invested their lives in ministry and have come to the end of their days with nothing to show for it, sometimes not even an inner satisfaction. Many have gone without to give to others, only to have others take advantage of them.

But if biblical standards don't apply, what are we called for? Watching and remembering some of our history helps.

A Golden Thread

Several hundred years ago Cotton Mather prayed for revival in New England. It came in the Great Awakening one year after he died. He never saw it. But God brought the revival.

In England, Anthony Ashley Cooper, the seventh Earl of Shaftesbury, worked to eliminate some of the horrible labor that was destroying children. As a committed Christian, he pushed Parliament for laws to protect children, urged the beginning of "ragged schools" to give the rudiments of education to poor children, and saw the end to what he called a "brutal iniquity" with the passage of an act that ended the exploitation of children. Shaftesbury, a privileged man by birth, did not see his wealth nor his benefit of class as something to use for himself but to help others. He is known as the pioneer of Christian philanthropy.

Five missionaries to the Aucas who were slain in 1956 couldn't have known that their refusal to use their weapons would mean that someday Auca Christians would also proclaim the gospel in dangerous surroundings, not fearing death. The Aucas know now that a believer will lay down his life to bring the message of new life to others.

There is a golden thread running through history. It is the thread of faithful people who by their sacrificial living for Christ have made it possible for us to hear about Jesus and believe.

We are debtors to them.

That's why we keep on giving, trusting the same One who used the giving of another person, years before, to bring the message of the Savior to us.

The faithful pastor of a struggling rural parish may be much more faithful to the will of God than the minister of a wealthy church in the suburbs who looks successful because of the increasing number of people moving into his community.

When a schoolteacher moved from the East Coast to teach in Michigan's rural Upper Peninsula, it took years before the wary Finnish settlers accepted the stranger. But he built a reputation as a good teacher and started a Sunday school. Twenty years later when he moved to a new location to start over again, he left behind a fellowship of believers able to carry on the gospel witness. Textbooks on church history will not mention this modern St. Paul. He is an unknown, ordinary man who gave up tenure, conference days and fringe benefits to work where others did not care to go. He did it for Christ. God knows the man and his work.

When a mother gives her hours to the care of a handicapped child, or an elderly woman takes on the responsibility of foster children, most people don't notice. Newspaper headlines rarely reveal the stories of the quietly faithful. But they influence lives.

Jesus Wouldn't Qualify

By some human standards Jesus was a failure. He was not successful in terms of owning a large house ("Foxes have holes and birds of the air have nests, but the Son of Man has no place to lay his head" Mt 8:20). He did not have titles or degrees. In fact, those who teach the gospel of riches can't use Jesus as an example of "one whom God has blessed." They could use Pilate—he was rich and had a big home—but not Jesus.

Our measure of obedience is not larger incomes, great successes or even pleasant experiences. Our call to serve doesn't come from the demands of the ego or the pull of the marketplace. Our directions come from another place.

Obeying the will of God means doing what he tells me to do in the way he tells me to do it. A cup of cold water given may not seem much when we read of those who dig wells to supply hospitals in the desert, but that cup of cold water might be given to the one who will himself some day dig wells in the desert. But even if he doesn't, I am called to give that cup of water.

Not Much, But Enough

It may not seem like much to speak to someone in prison, but who is that one in prison he is pointing me to? I don't have to know because God does.

It may not seem like much to spend ten minutes with a child, but God has control of her life too. I may be God's voice of direction or encouragement if I obey and invest that ten minutes.

Lowell Berry, a successful businessman, didn't have any money when he was taught to tithe as a little boy. But someone took time with him to teach him about biblical tithing. Years later, a wealthy man, he provided the expenses for thousands of pastors and seminarians at the Billy Graham Schools of Evangelism.

What does God want from me? He wants me to be open to him, to be willing to move in any way that he cares to have me go. The question has been asked: "What could God do with you if he were free to do anything he wished and you would obey?" Ponder that for a little while.

God is looking now for those who will ask, "What does God want from me anyway?" and then follow him no matter how unglamorous or unrewarding.

Finding the will of God does not mean our pathway

will be clear always or our future settled once and for all. There will be changes. We turn many corners. A missionary explained, "The leading of God is not usually a sharp turn. It is a curve angling slowly." There are few right-angle turns with God.

Sometimes in seeking honestly to obey we even make the wrong turn. But that doesn't stop God from leading us. He can push us back onto the right path, and he will. He knows exactly where we are now, and he knows where he wants us to be tomorrow.

3

When the Signals
Get Blurred

We've all heard it: "*I don't think this is the will of God for you.*" Or, "You aren't in the will of God."

Then we begin to wonder, "Am I?"

Can I really know what God has planned for me? There comes a time for all of us when God wants either to get us started in a new direction or to reconfirm a call that is getting a little weak. Some of the most exciting times in our lives, if we don't panic, are the times when we honestly try to follow the Lord and the signals get blurred. That's not a worry, that's an opportunity—if we're careful.

Marti grew up in a Christian home, knew all of the biblical answers about relating to men, and was all set for university life—or so she thought.

By her second semester she had battled out the problem of dating non-Christians, convinced that God wasn't going to bless a relationship that was combining darkness with light. She wanted a Christian. Then she found one.

He went to church, professed faith in Christ, but had ideas about virginity that went with what most of the non-Christians were saying. Still, he wasn't an unbeliever, she told herself. She was having fellowship with a believer—even though he was trying to get her into his bedroom.

Her roommate tried to warn her, but Marti didn't want to listen. She could control a man, she thought. Besides, what could her roommate know—she wasn't dating anybody. Two other Christian women tried to talk to her too.

She wrote them off as jealous.

Finally, three committed Christian men got to her. They sat her down in a corner of the dorm lounge and said bluntly, "We know this guy." Then they told her their own fears about where the relationship might be heading. They were loving, but they were also tough.

Marti cried. She told them that they didn't understand, that they didn't know him the way she did. But later, alone in her room, she admitted to herself and to God that her friends wouldn't have spoken as they did if they had not been praying or did not care about her.

She broke off the relationship, and still feels the pain of it—and loneliness. There is no one else. Sometimes she still wonders what might have been.

It was her friends, not Marti, who could see what

was happening. Her own emotions were getting in the way. And, even though these friends are now married and she has no one, she is still convinced that they were right.

Caught by Feelings

When the signals get blurred, we need one another. In the body of Christ we have many members—all relating to each other. Individuals are not capable of always understanding the will of God for themselves.

Those who try to understand God's will on their own too often get caught by their own feelings, sometimes confusing an adrenalin high with the inspiration of God. They look for signs, visions, sensations and even pick up the occult term *vibrations* to describe what they call the leading of God.

Some have a direct line to heaven, or so they think. They are in tune with God, and it leads them into all kinds of difficulties. They do not realize that Satan will give them any sensation they desire so long as he can lead them his way. Sooner or later they will trip and fall, and when that happens there is a tendency to quit on God, saying that God can't be trusted. What they mean, of course, is that they can't trust the feelings they thought were of God.

God doesn't want us to be confused. He wants us to know his plan for our lives. For people who want to discover his will, there are several avenues to follow.

The Best Interpreter of Scripture

Search the Word of God. Read the Bible every day and take notes. God's will never contradicts his own teaching in Scripture. Much confusion can be eliminated when we know what God is saying in his Word. If we get a "leading" that is contrary to the Bible, we can know without doubt that we are wrong—God does not contradict his Word.

The best interpreter of Scripture is more Scripture. The same Holy Spirit who inspired the writing of the Bible also inspires the reading of it. Knowing that we want to follow him, God's Spirit leads us through Scripture. We don't have to read with a panicky "O God, teach me, show me quick" attitude. We can relax with his Word, enjoy it and spend time daily pondering and reflecting as we read it. As we do, we will begin to be impressed by the ways he supplied needs in other people's lives and realize that he can do the same with us too. We discover an aspect of truth about him that we hadn't known before and sense that he wants us to apply that truth in our lives as well.

As we read, God's Spirit encourages, uplifts and demonstrates his love and leading by biblical examples as well as by defining the meaning of our discipleship. Through the Word we discover that the Bible's story parallels our own. The two-edged sword corrects and shapes us. Through God's Word we begin to feel and see the way he wants us to go as we walk along with him.

In reading Scripture, remember that the passage may not always have an immediate application. That doesn't matter. God is teaching, and like any lesson it may not be applied for years. Then at the right time, when it is needed, the lesson learned from Scripture will come back. Study the Word of God, hide it in your heart—and what you understand, obey.

Prayer—a Conversation, Not a Monolog

Another avenue for learning God's will is prayer. That sounds so simple that many people miss it. They say, "Of course," but they don't pray.

Prayer is a conversation, not a monolog. It isn't rushing into God's presence with a list of requests and then leaving. It is waiting on God. Keeping a daily appointment with him insures the gradual leading that is a certain and systematic way for the will of God to be revealed. Most of us can only assimilate and act on small portions of guidance at a time anyway. God knows that, so he is teaching and leading us in small steps as we are ready.

In prayer, reaffirm to God that you are his, that you do want to obey and will obey him. Ask him to show you if anything stands in the way of his leading you. If there is something, confess it and let him remove it.

The promises of God are exciting. He does not lie when he says, "If you ask anything in my name, I will do it" (Jn 14:14 RSV).

But how does God lead us through prayer? Do we hear voices, dream dreams, get a warm, fuzzy feeling, an inner excitement? How?

Fortunately, the way of his leading through prayer can't be completely explained. If it could, we would have all kinds of problems. Everyone would be checking against the yardstick. We'd all be comparing notes. We can't do that because we are all different. God made us and knows how to communicate his will to us. If there were specific rules or systems to be applied, prayer would no longer be a two-way communication. It would be signal receiving. God wants to communicate.

God leads in prayer in personal ways that give an awareness that "God has me!" As we pray, the experiences of his holding and guiding contribute to our understanding of how he specifically leads us. He knows how he does it, and after a while we start to know it too.

But all of our praying and seeking can't be done alone. We need each other! That's the reason for the fellowship of other Christians. That's the reason Scripture instructs: "Let us not give up meeting together, as some are in the habit of doing, but let us encourage one another" (Heb 10:25).

Tell your Christian friends what you are praying about, and they will pray with you. Then do the same with them. The most welcome words you can hear from someone are, "How can I pray for you?" A beautiful thing happens when two or more Christians pray together. Jesus said it would be so (see Mt 18:20), and he is right.

But there are some sad examples, unfortunately, of people who miss out on that blessing.

Two men, traveling for their company, visited a church on Sunday morning. During the prayer time worshipers were asked to share with one another their prayer requests.

One of the men turned to someone near him, found out that person's name and immediate need, and prayed for him. Then, that other person prayed for him. But the second man took that valuable prayer time to tell how important he was in his company. He never did get to pray—and there wasn't time for the other person to pray for him. He cheated himself, and he cheated that other church member. The first man went out of the church blessed and happy by the fellowship he enjoyed. The second man experienced nothing.

Take advantage of every opportunity to pray with others. Get a prayer partner, someone you can trust, and then pray together. The promise is there, "If two of you on earth agree about anything you ask for, it will be done for you by my Father in heaven" (Mt 18:19).

Going with the Circumstances

A third way to discover the will of God is through the circumstances God has put you in. He knows where you are and what your life situation is. He does not wish, as we sometimes do, that we were somewhere else. Some of the most faithful Christians are living in tough surroundings. They have picked up their leading from where they are and are doing great things for God.

This means you may find yourself in a situation that you can't do anything about. You can't control world economics or earthquakes, or even the decisions of people in immediate authority over you. But God knows your circumstances. You may feel at times that you are being buffeted as a reed in the wind and have no choice in matters affecting you. But not to have choices does not limit God. He will use what choices you have, the choices of others and the situations you are in. The leading will be there.

But often we do have some control over our circumstances, and that can actually cause problems if we are not careful. We can begin to respond to situations on the basis of our ego needs and think "this is of God." Although many Christians have found God's leading by the circumstances around them—not all have.

It sometimes happens, unfortunately, that we respond so quickly to circumstances that we become victimized by everyone and every situation around us.

The believer needs discernment. Satan would like to have us acting only as responders, always running and seldom accomplishing. God wants us to know what is happening around us and be in command of the circumstances.

People who have a need to be known as Christian workers or counselors of others often spin their wheels in busy work or in counseling because they respond too quickly to cries of help only to find months, even years, later that they are being consumed by the demands of a few people who manage to tie up ninety per cent of their time. It's a shock to some who fancy themselves heavily involved in counseling when a time study shows that their counseling is with the same few, week in and week out, who are not really open to help.

Jesus was always on top of the circumstances around him. He knew who he was and what his ministry was all about. In Luke 4:43, we read that he left the clamoring, needy crowd because "I must preach the good news of the kingdom of God to the other towns also, because that is why I was sent." He got up and left. He knew when to do that.

We need to know, before God, what our calling is and not dissipate our energies. We must be strong enough to respond to the real needs, not just the apparent ones.

Parents understand that. If a mother reacted only to the demands of her children, they would govern her. Out of love she decides what they need and gives it to them. She knows, not from the whining but from what she observes, that one child needs a little extra love and encouragement, while another needs discipline. She knows what they should eat and when they should go to bed—they don't decide that for themselves.

Christians, who are salt and light, do not just cast their offerings whenever or wherever there is a clamor. They prayerfully look and give. Sometimes the one who is saying nothing has the greatest needs, while the ones who are making the most noise should be passed over until they are ready to accept the real help that they need.

The inner leading and the outward circumstances around us come together so that we are giving, not letting circumstances take, our strengths and offerings. We begin to develop the mind of Christ in these matters.

The leading of circumstances starts to make sense as we mature in the Lord. To the new believer this may seem nebulous, but we can learn from each other and learn from the example of Jesus to respond in the most effective way to the circumstances into which God places us.

Your Friends Are Your Teachers
Finally, pay attention to the advice of other Christians, particularly those who are themselves earnestly seeking God's direction for their lives. Although bad advice is possible, it is less so in the abundance of counselors (Prov 11:14).

Many Christians have found their places of service in the world through the advice of other persons who saw the gifts that God had given them.

In some schools guidance seminars have replaced

guidance counselors. Faculty and students alike have realized that often peers can analyze the gifts and training of their friends better than anyone else.

At one session a graduating senior was urged to take a particular job because "we can really see you there." Fellow students told him, "The job requires the gifts that God has given to you. It seems to be exactly what God has been preparing you for."

It wasn't the direction that student would have chosen for himself. He did not feel ready. But after talking to these friends who knew him and could help him discern what God was doing in his life, he relaxed and took the post.

When a pastor left one position for another, he said, "Everything that I looked for was missing in that new position, but my wife said to me, 'You have the gifts that church needs.' " We can't always see it ourselves, so God speaks through others who can.

Being in God's will is an adventure in faith. The road may not always be comfortable, but it is right.

We all want easy answers about guidance, but there aren't any! Guidance is part of a relationship. It isn't a commodity that you get from the store.

What If You Still Don't Know?

What happens when we ask and pray, pay attention to the circumstances and seek the counsel of others, but still don't know?

Sometimes, even after we read the Bible to make sure we are not violating any of God's teachings, and pray by ourselves and with others, and talk with friends who love us and will counsel us, and observe the circumstances surrounding us—we still don't know if we are really in the will of God.

There is an answer that is so simple that many of us miss it. God *is* leading you. You want his leading and certainly he wants to lead you. The silence you get from him means that all is well—keep going.

Older Christians, with years of experience in the Lord, are able to recall that God was leading them— even when they didn't think so and there were no signals. With that as background, they continue on in trust.

But for most new Christians who haven't had the years of experience that prove to them that God does lead even when they don't feel led, the future is somewhat terrifying when they have to make a decision and have no idea at all what God is saying or doing.

We look for a Damascus Road experience, the dramatic bolt out of the blue. But that's our problem, not God's. Why should God have to do that for me? He doesn't have to prove himself to me. If he did it once, I would expect it all the time.

If I am seeking his will and sincerely want to be obedient, then I can be certain that he is leading right now. He doesn't have to say to me, "Did you notice? I'm leading you." He wants to lead—he is leading. He knows as well as I do that his will is the only way I can find fulfillment and peace.

No Dramatic Kicks

If I don't get a dramatic kick from God, that doesn't mean I am outside his will. It may mean the opposite— I may be on the right path now. He has to push me only when I stray. As long as I have my hand in his, he will keep on leading. I never have to worry about whether or not he is leading, only about my willingness to be led. Silence is action. As a Christian I can say with confidence, "God has me."

A young Christian said, "I get so discouraged not knowing."

A friend listening replied, "Yes, but you find you have learned so much more than if you had been hit on the head and told what to do."

That friend was right. We learn to do what the writer of Proverbs urged: "Trust in the LORD with all your heart and lean not on your own understanding; in all your ways acknowledge him, and he will make your paths straight" (Prov 3:5-6).

The most relaxed people in the world are the Christians who know that God is in control. They are not in a panic, demanding every moment that God show them he is in control. Believers do not need constant assurance of what is a fact.

Don't look for dramatic action from God. Rather, rest in the day-by-day peace of God. Don't demand that he prove his lordship. He doesn't have to.

Then, as the years go by, you will be able to look back and say, "He did have me."

Once we get over the idea of a dramatic leading and start to trust him, the resulting peace is beautiful.

But I Like It!

Another point has to be made here. There are a few misguided Christians who think, "I must be out of the will of God because I am enjoying myself." Or, "I am doing the very thing that I would choose to do; therefore, this can't be what God wants."

That's like saying God doesn't understand me or even like me. It's built on an assumption that if it's fun or I like it, it can't be of God.

But he made me and gave me my talents and abilities and likes and dislikes, and he assembled the whole combination that is "me." Most of all, he loves me.

If I have a talent for music and like it, why should I assume that I must keep on praying to God for a revelation of his will. Obviously he wants me to develop my music unless he very clearly tells me otherwise in such direct terms that I can't miss what he is saying.

There are times when God says, "Go this way"—and we had better go—but most of the time he says nothing because we are already going the way he wants us to go. We are using what we have the way he wants us to use it. There is no need for him to say or do anything more.

Try a little test. What would you do if you could do anything you wanted without regard for finances or time?

Just thinking about that sounds wrong. But that's because so many of us think we must try to push against the very nature God has given us. If God wants you to paint pottery, then go to it. As long as you are always available to him so that he can steer you down another road if he wants to, you are in the will of God.

There is another reason for usually going ahead with what we like. Many people, determining who they are and how they function and what gifts God has given to them, get started in something only to find that God has let them go that way so that they will accumulate the kinds of experiences that fit them for a different task that is still in the future.

God Doesn't Waste Anything

God is economical. He doesn't waste training or experiences. He knows what we are doing, what we are learning, and how he is going to use all of that five, ten, twenty years from now.

It's easy to be disappointed when we have prepared for "the plan of God for my life," only to have the door shut in our faces.

That's because we were busy focusing on the plan when God was focusing on the preparation. Watch how he uses that preparation in a whole new way.

When the signals seem to be blurred and you are uncertain, keep on praying, keep on getting Christian counsel, but don't stop what you are doing. Trust him to steer you if you are on the wrong course. But don't stop!

A sailboat's rudder is useless while the sails are down. Set sail, get going. You can't get any direction until the wind fills the sails. Then when the wind changes, be ready to come about. God may have to change your course, but when he does, you will have the momentum for it.

God knows how to move you when the time comes for you to be moved. He knows what is happening to you and what should be happening for you. In other words, trust God to be God. There isn't anything he doesn't know. Don't try to filter him through your own emotional system—or second-guess him.

Turn or Crash

There are people who refuse to alter course even when they know that God is making it clear that it's time to go in a new direction. They try to hang onto a job or an idea or a goal because what they have is more comfortable or certain than what may lie ahead. As a result, they are no longer available for what God really wants. In trying to hang onto some good thing they have now, they run the risk of missing God's best.

That even happens to dating couples. Both women and men sometimes find it easier to hang onto the person they are dating now than allow God to bring new people into their lives. Even those who are receptive to whomever God might bring along still prefer to hold onto the one person they have rather than be free for awhile to grow so that God can prepare them for his best. But following God's leading means responding to an inner awareness or counsel that a particular relationship isn't right. It means being willing to stay alone for as long as God wills rather than make a mistake. Those who have freed themselves to meet and marry the best that God has for them, or to go on into a single life of commitment, will find a life far more fulfilling than they dreamed possible.

Why doesn't God introduce the right two people to each other right away and save the painful experiences? Because no one is ready for marriage until he or she is ready to follow God's will. God's choice may not be ready for me yet. I may not be ready for God's choice. There is first a wholeness to be learned alone that equips us for a relationship with someone.

Only when I have wrestled with a willingness, even

a commitment to the single life, and surrender to God's will, am I ready for whoever God has for me, if indeed he has someone at all. A lot of people settle for a union. God wants his children who marry to enjoy marriage, which can only be possible in him. Only when God has first place in my life can he trust me with his kind of marriage or his kind of single life. Only when I come to that kind of surrender can I be ready for either marriage or a celibate life that opens up doors to larger service than most family people can enter.

Living on God's Terms

Both vocation and marriage, two of the major decisions that each of us makes, are serious to God. The key is to do what he wants on his terms so I can become the whole person he wants me to be and get the experiences he wants me to have. Then I can be ready for a specialized ministry, a vocation and possibly be presented to another person in marriage. Another immense benefit is added to this. I will have discovered a quality of satisfaction in him that nothing that I may want or take for myself can begin to match.

God is helping, refining and polishing us. He wants to do it. He is sure of his own leading. We can be sure too. God doesn't make mistakes.

4

Sometimes I Get Angry with God

Don't *be surprised if it happens! You may* find yourself angry with God.

Marilyn, a young woman, already appointed with her husband to their first term on the mission field, died in a car crash. Her husband is left alone now to care for an infant daughter. A lot of people are asking, "Why, God?"

When Bill was only a few weeks away from being made vice president of his company—a goal he had aimed for all his adult life—he was struck down by a heart attack.

Judy had her bridesmaids chosen, her wedding invitations printed and the church reserved, when her fiancé told her that he wasn't so certain any more, and would like to postpone the wedding—maybe permanently.

Little Scott died slowly of leukemia. His parents could only watch their son and pray. On their knees, they cried.

Life isn't fair. We are in a world of decay caused by the Fall. The result of sin touches every dimension of our being and the world around us. Sickness is here—and we will get sick. Corruption is here—and we will be hurt. Suffering is all around us—and it will invade our homes. The apostle Paul told us, "We know that the whole creation has been groaning as in the pains of childbirth right up to the present time" (Rom 8:22). Creation groans and we do too—but we are not alone. A few lines farther on the same author reveals God's help: "In the same way, the Spirit helps us in our weakness. We do not know what we ought to pray for, but the Spirit himself intercedes for us with groans that words cannot express" (Rom 8:26).

When the Questions Come

If you think you have everything figured out, that God is blessing your life and is giving you what seems to be even more than what you asked for, don't be surprised if suddenly everything crumbles. It happens, and when it does, it's a vicious blow.

That's when the questions come—and with the questions, anger.

It starts at first with a reverent, "Why?" Then, when no quick revelation comes or no reason can be fathomed, the bitterness starts to creep in. It helps to recognize it—and clear the air with God, because if you don't, it will eat at you like a cancer.

A Christian woman who seemed to have everything going wrong in her life tried to pray, but couldn't. Finally, she asked her friends to pray with her, so they tried. They started, stopped, and asked, "What's the problem? There's a block. We can't pray with you."

Then she admitted, "I'm angry at God."

She expected them to be shocked or to lecture her on how she ought to show proper respect and honor toward God. Instead she got a relieved, "Well, why didn't you say so. Tell him that you are angry so that you can get things settled."

They understood what she still had to learn—God knows when we are just saying words or playing prayer games with him. He knows when we are angry. Just as every husband or wife knows from icy comments or stony silence that their spouse is angry, so does God.

Settle Your Differences with God

In our human relationships, when we love someone, we know it and they know it. When we are angry with them, they know that too. Anger and love are really two extremes of the same emotion.

Settle your differences with God. Get them out where you can deal with them. Jesus said, "I have called you friends" (Jn 15:15). If two friends can't talk about what has come between them, something is wrong.

Anger that is brought out into the open can lead to reconciliation and restored harmony. Two people who argue and then settle the argument will often be closer than before because they have communicated honestly and neither is harboring unconfessed anger.

This is just as true with God as it is with the people we love. But if I want reconciliation, I have to be honest enough to say what is bothering me. Refusing to articulate anger is like saying loud and clear, "I don't want it cleared up. I like the wall separating us." That can't be if I love a person, and it can't be if I love God.

Dangerous Anger

There is a caution that must be given here. It is dangerous to be always angry with God. A person who fights with God puts himself up as an equal with God—in other words, as a rival! Some people like to fight, and they like to fight God. It gives them a sense of power. They are arrogant—they shake their fist at him.

A pastor who wanted to move to a larger church got his eyes off the ministry and onto the prestige and opportunities that a larger church could offer him. He wouldn't admit it though. In fact, he couched his wants in terms of "a better opportunity to serve the Lord."

But he wasn't even taking advantage of the opportunities he had to serve the Lord in the church where he was. He was miserable—always looking, never finding. When he learned that a large, prestigious church was seeking a pastor, he exploded, "Yes, but I bet they won't ask me."

He was angry with God, angry with those who have the responsibility of pastoral placement, and he took it all out on his congregation. He did less and less in the church.

Each Sunday instead of encouraging and teaching and feeding the flock in his church, he criticized them for being unspiritual, not caring. In short, he saw in them his own failures. Even his choice of words showed how he was projecting his own guilt: "You are not fulfilling the will of God for your lives."

The dismayed congregation was deeply hurt. People who were already doing far more of the ministry than the pastor, trying hard to fulfill the will of God in their lives, couldn't understand where they had fallen short. One woman said, "No matter what I do I am attacked for not doing more."

They didn't understand because the pastor who was attacking them didn't understand. He was angry with God, and instead of confessing it and getting things settled, he chose to hold onto his anger and attack the flock.

Instead of going to the Chief Shepherd to get his signals straight, he was biting and devouring and harassing the flock that was his charge. He was like a sheep dog, invaluable to the shepherd when he obeys the shepherd's signals, but destructive to the flock when he doesn't.

Slowly some of the parishioners began to recognize his problem. They knew that they had to support and love their pastor even as they also had to protect the congregation from his anger.

It was difficult, but members of the congregation, knowing the love of God in their own lives, kept him from hurting as much as they could while they loved him. In a way, they did just as a parent does for a child who is always most obnoxious when he needs love most.

A few people, not understanding how anger works, became bitter, found they couldn't love their pastor, and left the church—but only a few. The larger number did not depend on the man in the pulpit—they depended on the Lord and vowed to help.

The pastor was ministered to. Knowledgeable parishioners agreed that if the pastor did go to a different, larger or "better" church, he would be a happier servant of Christ if they took the responsibility to help him become a better minister before he moved. They knew that if he did move elsewhere, he would have learned some valuable lessons and wouldn't hurt another congregation too.

Their love began to bring results. As his anger mellowed, God was able to bless him through his parishioners, and the church began to be a family again.

Going for Reconciliation

When a Christian is angry with God, he can do a lot of harm to others. It takes a supportive group of believers to help him see that it is far worse to hide the causes of anger and react in hurtful ways than it is to go to the Lord and talk it over with him.

Going for reconciliation means we want to be reconciled. When that happens, beautiful results can come.

God wants me to be free enough to say outright, "There is something between us and I am unhappy about it." God doesn't want grudges harbored.

When things have gone wrong, or just seem to be wrong, confession opens the door to seeing things from God's perspective—that it isn't my plans, my goals, my ambitions or desires that need to be blessed, but my relationship to him.

When I want God more than I want any of the things

I pray about, a new and deeper peace overshadows any of the goals I may have set for myself. That discovery not only resolves my anger with God, it shows me why I tend to become angry with him.

Do I want him more than I want anything else? Is anything in the way of that? Will I be angry with him for not giving me what I thought we both wanted for me? Can I love him more than anything else so that I will stay in fellowship with him no matter what comes of it?

No Matter What

Am I willing to want the will of God, no matter what it costs, even if I can see nothing but unhappiness ahead?

Separated by half a continent, an engaged couple met individually with concerned, mature Christian friends about their marriage plans. Both wanted to marry the person God had chosen for them, and they thought they had found that one in each other. Yet, both were a little uncomfortable.

Their friends, independent of what the other partner's friends were saying, explained that they were not ready for marriage. Both came to a realization—painful as it was, and they both cried many nights—that they were to seek the will of God first no matter whether God would have them marry or remain single the rest of their lives. It was not an easy conclusion for them. For a while, both struggled and fought with God.

But when they came to the conclusion that God is God and must be first, and began to live that out in their lives, then, and only then, did God begin the process that brought them back together. Only this time it was around himself.

Today they are happily married to each other, and time has shown that God was preparing each for the other in such a unique way that they are indeed perfect for one another.

Well, then, why did God allow them to go through so much pain?

Why indeed? Except that he used it to show them himself and help them understand, even though it was painful, that he loves them far more than they could ever love each other. They were planning a wedding, but that's all it was. When they were willing to give each other up to obey God, they discovered the meaning of the phrase, "God reserves the right to give us something better than what we ask for." God has united them in himself—it is a beautiful marriage.

Anger That Leads Somewhere

Job didn't like what was happening to him either. He became angry, but even in his anger he admitted to God, "You are God." He discovered, "He is not a man like me that I might answer him, that we might confront each other" (Job 9:32). And he never forgot it.

God blessed Job's life just as he wants to bless each life that belongs to him. Sometimes we get so caught up in the theological discussion of the intervention of Satan in Job's life that we miss the divine-human element. God knew Job and had his hand on him all the time.

God doesn't want me to be miserable! Being human, I assume that therefore everything will be easy with no pain—but not so. Sooner or later each of us comes to realize that there will be pain all life long but that God's grace is sufficient for it. Job went through a rough time, but, anger and all, he went through it with God.

Anger is not bad if it leads somewhere. People who pretend that they are never angry are usually just pushing their anger inside. Anger is normal—it is a human emotion.

Some Christians, not wanting to admit to anger because they think it is unchristian, explain away the anger they feel but want to deny. Justifying themselves, they claim the example of Jesus who threw the moneychangers out of the Temple. When they express anger at injustice, evil in government, or people involved in pornography or abortion or drugs, they call it righteous anger. It is real anger, and it is understandable, but there is a subtle danger in their classification of it. They forget something—none of us is righteous. None of us sees things with the clarity of the divine mind. Though we are adopted as children of God we are not *the* Son of God.

All of us tend to filter things through our own emotions. We get upset and lash out at what bothers us. We cater to our own pet peeves. We need to understand our tendencies so that we do not simply assume that what is upsetting us is also upsetting God and that our anger is like his—righteous.

We may think we are angry about the same things that anger him, but we risk the danger of putting ourselves in the place of deciding for God what angers him. We end up trying to be God.

There are also Christians who react angrily to people

and circumstances around them because they are just plain angry people. They need to blast something or someone. It's an outlet.

Some of us who love Christ are seen by the public as haters of people because we have acted in angry, hateful ways or because we have thought that we could dogmatically and angrily defend our views as God's views. Some are seen as hateful people because in emphasizing the soul we are seen as contributors to the pain of people. There are Christians who witness for souls but care little to help others in need. Persons who gravitate to liberation theology are not necessarily always drawn by socialistic or Marxist views so much as they are driven to react to narrow, bigoted, even hateful views of some who claim to follow Christ but grasp, use, consume and thus injure their fellows. It is a sad and costly anger that some express.

When We Try to Be Balanced
It is easy to get Christians who cannot agree on doctrine or church polity or even scriptural interpretation to become united around anger. There is a quality of "fellowship" to it. There are leader types who capitalize on anger, building a fellowship around whatever they are angry about. And usually they call their anger righteous too. But knowing the mind of Christ means being like him—balanced in our thinking.

A balanced Christian follows Jesus. When anger does come, it's not his own as much as a reflection of Christ in him. Christ faces the sin in people in order to purge out evil as he sees it. Not only does he call people to new birth and the resulting new nature so that they can be different, he calls people who are already believers to practice what they were saved to be and to stop getting their directions from the world.

But it isn't easy. Try to correct people, and you won't always be loved for it. We sometimes think that if we are peacemakers the warring parties will love us. But in fact what usually happens is that neither side loves us, because they want us to agree with them and be in their camp. They will reject anyone who is not one hundred per cent with them on their terms.

Jesus came "to preach good news to the poor, . . . to proclaim freedom for the prisoners and recovery of sight for the blind, to release the oppressed, to proclaim the year of the the Lord's favor" (Lk 4:18-19). That's our purpose too.

There are Christians who take only the first part about preaching and then spiritualize the second part, assuming that their job is only to talk the good news. They do little else for people. Then they angrily criticize other Christians who care about releasing the captives and helping the oppressed as being less spiritual. They make a category out of the term *humanism,* not realizing that good people who care about helping people considered humanism to be a love and a respect for fellow human beings. Making humanism a pejorative term can classify us as people haters. No Christian must be seen as a people hater. God hates sin, not people. His followers do the same.

Other Christians take only the second part of Luke 4:18-19 and assume that they are following Jesus if they get involved in the release of captives, healing and social concerns, but they never preach Christ as the Savior who sets people free. They are often critical, even angry, at those who do. They have not moved into an obedient walk with Christ in the whole ministry that he practiced.

Maturing Christians are balanced in their response to Jesus and balanced in their response to the world. They are not simple-answer people, easily captured by the rhetoric of the world even when it creeps into the church.

For example, when mature Christians look at racism—and there is racism in every part of the world—they do not gravitate to one camp or another. They will not tolerate the hateful racial slurs of whites toward blacks. But neither will they react and go the other way and slander whites. They will not be white racists nor will they be black racists. They will see people's sins, not racial sins. They will not be forced into buying the package of any slander group. They stand against racism—wherever it is—and work to eliminate it. They respond to every social, personal or ecclesiastical sin that way, but they won't buy into slogan groups—either right wing or left wing—who base a lot of their reactions to the world not on Scripture but on their own anger.

Legitimate Anger

Legitimate anger comes when we begin to see things as God's people, a people saturated with his teachings. If our will is to do his will, the cause of our anger will be the cause for our action. He will stop us if we are wrong.

We do get angry at government officials who spend money for their own political goals at the price of injuring the country. We do react against those who are self-seeking but do not represent their constituency.

We campaign, we speak out, we get involved in political parties—though always careful not to sell out to a party, because we are already sold out to Christ. We work as Christians to bring into office responsible leaders.

We do become angry at a labor union representative who will cheat management or his own coworkers if it means improving his own position or bank account.

We get angry and we do act. But not because we are antiunion or prounion but because we are representatives of the Light of the world. The position of Jesus is clear—and so is ours—to thwart evil.

We do get angry when we see business leaders and financial officers bleeding their workers or cheating the public. We get angry and we speak out, but not because we are antibusiness or probusiness, or because there is gain for us personally. We get angry because we've read the Bible and know what Jesus said and recognize that we are his ambassadors. Someone must speak out in the name of God.

It does anger us to see the flight to the suburbs of people, even Christians, who want to leave the inner city and then at the same time encourage their highway departments to rip out homes and uproot families who can't move, destroying communities in order to build concrete expressways to their own jobs in the city. They take real estate for roads, leaving residents in the inner city without the tax base needed for good schools. Because they are personally unaffected by the result, they won't even sympathize with "that slum problem."

Caring and Responding

Caring Christians go to city planning meetings and council sessions. Like those before us who fought against child labor, slavery, unjust taxes or tyrants in government, we respond as agents of the King against the systems and attitudes that hurt people.

We do become angry and speak out about the sexual abuse of children, murder in the womb, drug trafficking, sexism, cheating and all that hurts people. We ignore Luke 4 if we do not. The disciple must follow his master.

To those who ask, "How do you know that it is the will of God for you to speak out?" we can reply, "We know it is not the will of God that we remain silent." The Bible says, "Whoever knows what is right to do and fails to do it, for him it is sin" (Jas 4:17 RSV).

Of course, there are Christians who march, petition, argue and fight over an issue, but only when it affects them personally or touches their own pockets. The Christ-centered person cares about the plight of others, even when he is untouched personally, whether they live across the street or on the other side of the globe.

To be angry is to say, "I care." To ignore a person or need or situation is to say, "I don't care." Anger says, "I do care." And Christian anger says, "God cares too."

Retarding the Decay around Us

Anger based on the righteousness of Christ demands that the believer be as salt in the world, retarding the decay that is all around. It means the believer is a light pointing people to the one solution to all of the reasons for anger, the Lord Jesus Christ.

Some Christians look at things that should arouse

their anger and say, "Praise God anyway." They either pretend that something doesn't hurt or assume that all that is happening is what God wants. After all, "If God wants to stop it, let him stop it." In other words, "What will be will be." Scripture is true: "I know that everything God does will endure forever; nothing can be added to it, and nothing taken from it. God does it so that men will revere him" (Eccles 3:14). And it's true that "We know that in all things God works for the good of those who love him" (Rom 8:28).

But easy quoting of Scripture can also be a back door left open to irresponsibility. We are to balance the Word with the Word. The best corrective for an unbalanced view of Scripture is more Scripture.

Sometimes we label things "God's will" when it is really a Satanic activity. There is evil in the world. It's all around us.

It influences all of us, and it isn't of God. Evil comes in the form of sickness, death, pain and corruption, and all of it comes because we are in a fallen world. Satan is "the ruler of the kingdom of the air" (Eph 2:2). He "prowls around like a roaring lion looking for someone to devour" (1 Pet 5:8). We are in that world, and Satan is real.

There is pollution around us because of the grasping sin of people. There is war around us because of the hate in people. There is crime and corruption because of the evil in people's lives. We cannot say, "What will be will be."

There is social, political, spiritual and physical disease around us, and Christians are just as affected by it as anyone else because they are in the world too. Christians believe God cares and that he can heal, but they don't deny their anger at the very fallenness that made that disease.

If Christians are angry, they are to be angry in Christ. It's not an anger that is self-centered or enjoyed. It is an anger motivating them to do something. It is an anger motivated by love. Anger apart from love is egocentric. It comes out of and generates sin. Love that is anger is not proud anger, it is sad anger—but it is real.

While the world is in its sin, we continue to be the redemptive, healing community, redeeming in the name of Jesus whenever and however we can. Anger and love trigger us to do it. It's anger because we see and know and understand, not anger because of our weak human frailties that pitch us around on every wave, or influence us by every piece of gossip or newspaper story. We are angry because we are part of the body governed by the mind of Christ. He is the Head, and we care about the things he cares about. We love with the love of God who lives in us. It is his love, the love of the One who is "Christ in you" (Col 1:27). It is the love of the One of whom John said, "For God so loved the world that he gave his one and only Son, that whoever believes in him shall not perish but have eternal life" (Jn 3:16).

When God calls us to himself, we stand on holy ground. That's an awesome and responsible place to be.

5

I Seem to Have a Talent for Making a Mess of Things

Sandy was scared!

She knew what she might be getting into when she agreed to go out with him. She even broke another date with a man she trusted to go out on this one. But going against every Christian conviction in her that screamed, "Stop!" and pushing aside a promise she had once made to God, she told her trusted date that she was busy, knowingly went out with the man whose reputation preceded him—and did the very thing she had advised other women not to do.

Fortunately she was spared the pregnancy she feared. With tears in her eyes she gave thanks to God for deliverance and promised never to compromise again.

But her battle wasn't over. She still had to come to understand an important truth for emotional and spiritual freedom. Just as David once did, she prayed, "Create in me a clean heart, O God; and renew a right spirit within me" (Ps 51:10 KJV). As the weeks went by she was able to realize the position she had as a child of God. It is a place of status. She knew the promise applied to her that those who confess their sins are forgiven by God (1 Jn 1:9). She could now forgive herself.

Even though she had taken her Lord's name, the name she wore as a Christian, and had knowingly dragged that name with her into sin, yet like David, when she cried out and was delivered, then also like David she was able to go on with her Lord.

Taking Satan's Lure

Some of us wonder with Sandy why it is that "I have a talent for making a mess of things."

For one week every year I go fishing in Minnesota. I try a variety of artificial lures to catch walleyes and northerns.

Some days the fish strike one lure, some days another. But there is one particular lure that they go for every time. They can't resist it. That lure is chewed where so many fish have fought to dislodge the hook but couldn't. Those fish have a weakness, and I know what it is. Because I know, I can catch them.

Satan knows the weakness of every one of us too. He has a lot of different lures to dangle in front of us and may try them. But for each of us, he has a favorite lure and he knows how to use it.

Occasionally a fish will pull loose, ripping its skin, and with mouth hanging down it goes off to heal. But the scars will always be there. Sometimes we can pull

away from Satan too, but not before some painful tear-
ing occurs causing scars that will remain for the rest of
our lives. For even when we are made whole again by
receiving and accepting forgiveness, the physical and
sometimes the emotional results of what we did won't
go away. Christians get emotionally, physically and spiritually hurt, and they hurt others too.

There are so many painful ways for the people of God
to stumble, and Satan knows every one of them. As he
studies believers, he knows that he probably cannot
make us denounce Christ—but he can tempt us into a
compromise with sin. Satan knows exactly how to make
each one of us fall. Our weaknesses are no secret to him.

Knowing what we are like and how our minds work,
Satan will aim where we are vulnerable. A person may
not be tempted with greed, but might be tempted with
the pride that grows out of not being greedy. The person
who can't stand the taste of liquor will probably not
become an alcoholic—but he might lust for food. Satan
knows how to get to our weak spots. He knows where
they are.

Three things are certain about messing up our lives.
First, we don't have to yield to temptation. God has
made a way of escape. Second, if we do slip we don't
have to wallow in our mistakes. There is deliverance.
Third, we can use the lesson learned from falling not
only to avoid falling again, but to help some other person who is facing similar pressures.

Alone with Our Fantasies

Most temptations come because we are open to being
tempted. In solitude, when no one else is around, we

daydream. Our fantasies make us wonder what if, or what would it be like, or suppose I did. Then we begin to rationalize that it is probably okay, or we need this as part of our understanding of the way the world works. We can justify anything when we think about it long enough, even to the point of saying, "Well, God made me and knows my inner urgings," or, "It can help me be a more informed Christian."

One minister who took a strong public stand against pornography enjoyed reading the very magazines he condemned. When two women in his congregation found a stack of magazines hidden behind his filing cabinet in the church office, he tried to tell them that he was doing sermon research. The well-thumbed collection indicated a different kind of interest than just sermon preparation.

A denominational official who campaigned against massage parlors in his community financed some of his own illicit relationships with women through church missionary funds that were channeled through his office. He soon found that his secret was no secret at all, and the mission funds dried up as churches began to send their money directly to the missionaries on the field, not through his office.

It is easy to rationalize our sins, and Satan knows it. The teaching, "If I want it, I must need it," is one of Satan's favorite tricks.

Nevertheless, the committed Christian does have a way of escape. The Scripture has been verified in thousands of lives: "No temptation has seized you except what is common to man. And God is faithful; he will not let you be tempted beyond what you can bear. But when you are tempted, he will also provide a way out so that you can stand up under it" (1 Cor 10:13).

Run Away
We don't have to give in to temptation just because it comes. Jesus Christ provides a way of escape. Sometimes we have to get with other people and stay with them for support, or even run away from the temptation as Joseph did. If we do sincerely want to escape, we will find that there are friends who will care for us, even people who will stay with us.

One new Christian, still troubled by the pulling temptation of drugs, always calls his Christian friends to come and stay with him for a while when he gets depressed. He knows that his depression could drive him back into drugs.

Activity helps too. Roman Catholic seminary students are using practical wisdom when they spend their spare time on athletics rather than allowing themselves time for their minds to wander.

And proclaiming who we are keeps us safe. Oswald Hoffmann, well-known Lutheran clergyman, once reminded a group of ministers that they will less likely fall into sin if they wear their clerical garb. All of us who have put on Christ find the outward demonstration of that fact has a built-in safety feature (Rom 13:13-14).

Still, most of us have asked, "What if I slip? Do I have to give up and stay in my sin?" And someone always adds, "You don't know how far I've gone."

God Wants Us Back
No matter where we are coming from, all the evidence

at hand says clearly, God wants us back. The story of the prodigal son proves that. God's love does not depend on what an older brother thinks—he cares only that we come back. He counsels and draws us with the love in his own heart, a love that wants us home. That love has him out on the road waiting. He may be waiting for someone you know right now. He may be out there on the road waiting for you.

One of the most difficult questions Christians ask is, "How can I know that I am forgiven?" They quote passages such as Hebrews 6:4-6, 10:26-27 and 2 Peter 2:20-22 as evidence that they may have gone so far from God that there is no longer any hope for their return.

No one but God, of course, can say where backsliding ends or outright rejection of Jesus begins, but one thing is clear: if we are asking about coming back, then we are concerned—and if we are concerned, we are two-thirds of the way home.

Some people, having fallen, worry that even if God forgives them they will not be welcomed back by fellow Christians. If other believers in the fellowship do not welcome the erring one back, then their sin is worse than the fallen. In every church congregation there are people who have fallen and come back. Whether they stay and go on with Christ or get wounded again by condemning Christians depends on the attitude of the members of that Christian family. It must break God's heart when someone who is already broken gets beaten or stoned by those who take pride in their own wholeness. Jesus said, "By this all men will know that you are my disciples, if you love one another" (Jn 13:35 RSV).

Different People

We are hurt, and the whole body of Christ is hurt, when we act like renegades. Anyone who has gone his own way in opposition to God will recognize the warning signs and change course quickly.

When we are restored, God can and often will use our prodigal experience to help someone else. But he will do it only when he can use that experience in his own way, not when we call attention to ourselves.

There is a need for caution here. Part of the difficulty in welcoming home a brother who has fallen comes when that brother wants not only fellowship but leadership. Satan knows who the Christian leaders are and he has been successful in tripping some of them. Then, when loving Christians have helped the fallen one to his feet, the recovering one has asked for and has often been given his old place of leadership again. Then both the world and the church find themselves asking, "Has God no standards?"

Paul wanted John Mark as his associate and shows the love of one Christian for another in asking for his help even though John Mark had once failed. But Paul did the asking. From what we know about Paul's instructions for appointing leaders ("Do not be hasty in the laying on of hands," 1 Tim 5:22), he would not have requested John Mark had that younger man been pushy or arrogant or assumed that he had the right to be a leader once again.

When a twenty-five-year-old woman left her Christian upbringing, she made a conscious effort to go against all she had been taught. But when she returned, feeling the ugliness of her purposeful sin, she redeclared her faith in Christ, went home to her clergyman father and hugged him. She is accepted and loved but she still has years of planting her roots in Christ to be strong, dependable and eventually a mature leader.

We are called to be compassionate, called to have the mind of Christ which is a forgetting forgiveness, but as the Master did with Peter, we make the appointments to leadership on the basis of repentance and recommitment—not on the basis of ego or demand.

The Trap of Telling All

There is another reason to be careful. Some weak Christians vicariously enjoy the sins of others. There are weak Christians who like to listen to the testimonies of people who have plunged deeply into immorality. They invite the prodigal Christian to "share his testimony." They call it "marveling at the wonderful grace of Jesus." Actually, they are enjoying sin, fantasizing, vicariously committing the same sins in their minds.

That's why a Christian who has fallen away from the Lord and has then come back into fellowship has to be careful that he is not pulled into the publicity trap of telling all and letting others savor it.

If you are a restored Christian, say nothing! The time will come when God will trust you and use your experience to draw others to himself. Quietly, he will bring people to you for counsel. People with the same weakness or with the same sin will start crossing your path. You will not plan it or arrange it or even seek it. In God's timing it will "just happen."

It's a special gift, a mark of his blessing, to be used to help other people. God wants to do it through you.

But he won't do it if you start pointing to your dramatic release from gross sin rather than to the One who did the releasing. If God uses you to counsel, remember that he is the real Counselor who is allowing you to share in the experience of seeing another person restored.

Some people, reading something like this, may childishly think that they should go ahead and sin more, so that God can do more in their lives when they are forgiven. They may think they will have a more effective ministry because of their experiences in sin. It doesn't happen that way.

God is a forgiving God, but he is not soft in the head. Only when we weep over our own sins can we weep with someone else over his. Only when we can feel and agonize with another—just as someone once did with us—can we begin to be helpful and used of God.

Men and women of spiritual strength know that except for the grace of God they would still be lost. They do not capitalize on that—instead they allow God to use the fruits of his grace as he wills. Only God knows how to deal with someone who has fallen anyway.

None of us knows what the other person is going through even when it seems we have gone through the exact same thing ourselves. Because people are different, even the same experience has a different effect on people.

Channels by God's Choice

But the Holy Spirit, working within the other person and within us, can listen and speak. God will use us as channels for his healing, redemptive work. Even from our own wretched experience in sin God can bring a redeeming blessing for others. But only as God chooses to use it.

Occasionally there are arguments that if a Christian sins he probably wasn't a Christian to begin with. Maybe so, maybe not. It really doesn't matter.

Whether we are coming back to Christ or coming to Christ for the first time, the prayer of commitment is the same—a confession of sin, a calling on the Lord for deliverance and a willingness to submit to the lordship of Christ. We must come to the point where we can say, "I have been crucified with Christ and I no longer live, but Christ lives in me" (Gal 2:20).

Whether it is the new birth or a return to the Father after falling away, the child coming home does just that—comes home. With nothing in hand, like a child, waiting and ready to receive forgiveness.

And when we receive that forgiveness, we are no longer enemies, but beloved friends. And being loved people, we love him with everything that is within us.

Never again will we want to do anything that will separate us from his love. That's why having been close to God and wandered away and then returned again, we know that he and he alone is our source of love, joy and peace. We no longer try to determine the direction of our own lives. The living God, and he alone, plans our lives and lives within us each day. We want him to and that makes us new people.

We are no longer confused about who we are. We are his. We no longer wonder where we are going. We are going with him.

6

What about My Tomorrows?

Think *back five years.*

Would you have dreamed five years ago that you would be where you are now, doing what you are doing today? Would you have anticipated the world events or economic changes that are happening now? None of us can plan our lives, because we can't plan the direction of the world.

We can't anticipate our tomorrows. Those who do not know the One who owns tomorrow are left to face the future alone. But even though we who do believe cannot see into the future, we know the God who owns us and our future.

We don't negate ourselves when we trust in God who knows tomorrow. Rather it is a realization of self and the weaknesses that we carry into each day. It is also an understanding of who God is.

As God plans our tomorrows, he uses what he put into us—our gifts, our experiences, our education—and will tie it all together if we are faithful to what he is doing with us today.

It Happened to Me
I was a pastor in New Jersey and a graduate student in counseling when I was invited to become a campus minister at Michigan State University. It seemed an answer to prayer—both for the opportunity to work with students (a real love) and also because I could continue the same graduate studies at Michigan State.

But when I moved, that graduate program in counseling was dropped by the university. There was no chance to use my educational credits for a degree. At first this was bewildering. Then I saw what God had done. The practical experience of my psychology courses, gained through clinical counseling, was exactly what I needed for student ministry in those days of campus unrest during the Vietnam War. No one but God could have planned that for me. As a result, many young people not only came to faith during those years but got their own sense of direction and are serving Christ faithfully today.

Not knowing what else to do, yet wanting to keep my hand in academic work, I searched for a degree program at Michigan State and finally followed the advice, "Why don't you study journalism?" That didn't make much sense to some people—a master's degree from a seminary and a master's degree in journalism from a university are a strange combination, but it did seem to be an open door and there was no other leading.

One week after finishing the master's thesis, my first book was in process; the second followed right after that. Then, invitations to write came from magazine editors faster than I could accept them. In each case the editors were looking for those two areas of training— theological education and journalistic skills. Yet, all during the days of classroom work there was no evidence except an inner peace that this was the will of God for me.

Don't Rush Ahead
God knows what he is doing in our lives and does not have to take time to explain it all to us. He leads quietly, efficiently and in the end puts it all together for us in such ways that we could never arrange or figure out.

It is not God's way (probably because we could not handle it) to reveal his will too early. In his wisdom, he works out the details in our lives and in the lives of other people so that he can bring all the parts together. His will blesses each person he touches in every dimension of life.

And what if we decide to run ahead of God? Not only can we become ensnared in our own plans, we can hinder the blessing for someone else who is trusting and waiting, and whose answer lies partially with how God is working in us.

To rush ahead is to doubt the ability of God to handle our affairs. He knows our needs and how to care for us best. To shoulder him aside is to say, "I'll be God for me because I understand me best. I understand tomorrow better than you do, God."

That is an attempt to usurp God's place, and a few mistakes, plus the hurt that follows, prove that it doesn't work. After trying to run his own life, one college junior explained the folly when he said, "I guess it takes a couple of years to find out where all the dead ends are."

Our Own Careful Planning

When a young family bought their first house, they began to enjoy the feeling of security it offered as the property appreciated in value. It appeared to be just the financial cushion they needed for their basic net worth portfolio. They carefully painted and patched and improved the house. They added a recreation room and every few weeks looked at the real estate ads to check sale prices on comparable houses. They liked what they saw.

Then the Highway Department projected a six-lane freeway right through their neighborhood. Their property value fell 30% and they have a pollution-fomenting freeway outside their living room.

When the bitterness and the "Why, God?" questions settled, they had to admit that the house may have been too important to them. In subtle ways the house was offering to provide them with what no piece of real estate can ever guarantee—security.

Unfortunately, for most of us it takes something like that to happen before we can agree with Scripture that no one can pronounce, " 'Today or tomorrow we will go to this or that city, spend a year there, carry on business and make money.' Why, you do not even know what will happen tomorrow" (Jas 4:13-14). There is only One who is certain about tomorrow. He can be trusted. That doesn't mean we sit quietly and do nothing. It does mean that we walk closely with the Christ who lives in us.

When a U. S. government worker quit his job in Washington, D.C., to return to a rural lifestyle, he told friends that they had better not count on having a Social Security System when they retire. For some this created anxiety and even fear, others became angry about paying in money with no assurance that it would ever provide old-age benefits for them. But Christians who have a different concept of security can relax and keep on making their Social Security payments knowing that they can never rely on any future structure or government anyway. The only sure foundation is the Lord himself. And their present payments are helping others now.

Getting Away from Frustration

A Ph.D. candidate at a Midwestern university struggled to get his degree. He played the political departmental lobbying games, got trapped into "must" visits to the right faculty homes, bought the right number of drinks for the right faculty people at the clubs, and attended the right departmental functions and parties. Spiritually, he gave all of his time and self to the completion of his dissertation. Worship and witness went on the shelf.

But when he finally got the degree, he was miserable. He had hoped that it would give him status; it didn't even help him get a job. Then, slowly, as he watched others who had gone the same route and were continuing to work the angles (one even divorced his wife because she had not kept up academically and was a professional liability), he realized what was happening. He came back to his roots and through counseling and prayer rediscovered that only God can rule his life and his tomorrows.

Frustration dogs the steps of any Christian who having chosen to be a slave of Christ insists on planning the life he will have within that slavery.

Yet we do care about investments and planning and savings for the future because if we don't make provision for our families, we're guilty of disobedience to the Scripture. "If anyone does not provide for his relatives, and especially for his immediate family, he has denied the faith and is worse than an unbeliever" (1 Tim 5:8). If I do not work hard for the future, I am a sluggard. But I don't count on only what I do to secure my future.

Having created me, saved me and called me to himself, God doesn't just leave me to uncertainty about the tomorrows that I can neither control nor understand. He wants to help me with my tomorrows. God's word to exiles in Babylon is no less his word today: " 'For I know the plans I have for you,' declares the LORD, 'plans to prosper you and not to harm you, plans to give you hope and a future' " (Jer 29:11).

You Can Talk to the Heartknower

In Britain, with unemployment high and mine closings making the future even more bleak, there are young adults who have never held a job since leaving school and have no prospects for having one. They are victims of an economic situation that is out of their hands. Yet during the three-year ministry known as Mission England with Billy Graham, thousands of these young people were publicly stepping out to declare faith in Christ—and this in places where church attendance had been in decline. They had come to a realization—forced upon them but no less real because of it—that no economy, no social program, no government, nothing can give assurance. There is only One who cares about tomorrow because only One loves enough to care.

Tucked away in the Old Testament, in a book too often ignored, is a revealing passage of Scripture. "For the eyes of the LORD range throughout the earth to strengthen those whose hearts are fully committed to him" (2 Chron 16:9). God is always looking for ways to support us if our hearts are fully committed to him. We sometimes say, "Where is God? I can't find God. God is not close. God doesn't see." But he is close and he does see.

Psalm 139:18 goes even farther. It says he's up all night watching. Whether I sleep well or am pacing the floor most of the night, God is awake—watching me, paying attention to my needs. It has always been that way. "My frame was not hidden from you when I was made in the secret place. When I was woven together in the depths of the earth, your eyes saw my unformed body. All the days ordained for me were written in your book before one of them came to be" (Ps 139:15-16). God neither slumbers nor sleeps.

Everything is open before him. He sees everything that I do. Peter in his first letter (3:12) picks up a verse from Psalm 34:15, "The eyes of the LORD are on the righteous and his ears are attentive to their cry." God listens as a parent listens to a child, bending down his ear close, paying attention, looking into the child's eyes, hands on the child's shoulder, intently concentrating on what the child is saying. That's the way God is with us.

There is a part of 2 Chronicles 16:9 that talks about our hearts being fully committed to him. That's critical. God knows the heart—yours and mine. In our English translations Acts 15:8 begins, "God who knows the heart." But it's really like one word: "heartknower." God is the heartknower. You can talk to the heartknower, open yourself to the heartknower, trust the heartknower.

"What about tomorrow?" That's an unknown—no one but God can answer. But the question, "What about God?" is a known—anyone can answer. God guides tomorrow, and he is willing, indeed desires, to guide us. The question is not, "Will he?" The question is, "Will we allow him that opportunity in our lives?"

7

Peace—Getting It and Keeping It

Never will I leave you" (Heb 13:5).
Never?

Can we really believe that?

God promised it, but it isn't easy to trust in a blanket promise like that, not when life gets rough. And sometimes life can get very rough.

In our daily living, there is rarely any visible or tangible sign that God is right there with us. Yet, when we move along through life trusting his promises, and then look back, we find that he has kept his word. He did have every situation in hand.

That's enough to go on, and equips us to say, "Lord, you handled things before. I'll trust you to handle things again." And, once more, he does.

Some people, struggling to find the kind of peace that only God can give, trust themselves or their own clever maneuvering to get it. That doesn't work. Columnist Ernest Howse, writing in the *Toronto Star,* gave an example of someone who tried:

"In the gloomy years leading up to World War II, a wealthy man in Australia foresaw with fear the coming events which were casting their shadows before.

"He concluded that war was inevitable, that it would spread across the world, and that it would bring unprecedented horror and destruction.

"So he studied how he could find a safe hideout where he could spend his remaining years isolated from the dreadful reach of the approaching conflict.

"He made an extensive survey of geographical possibilities, and he finally settled on an idyllically remote and lovely retreat, a tiny and sparsely populated island in the Pacific.

"The name of the island was Guadalcanal."

Of course, before World War II was over, Guadalcanal became the scene of one of the most destructive bombardments of the Pacific war.

Running for our own shelter will never bring us peace. Every one of us, however, has met people who have found real peace even amid horrible circumstances by leaning back in trust on Jesus.

And, when they get it, the result is indescribably beautiful.

Watch a mature Christian die. Work with a handicapped Christian on a project. Spend a day with the Christian mother of a child with a terminal disease—you'll see it. They verify what Jesus promised: "Peace I leave with you; my peace I give you. I do not give to you as the world gives. Do not let your hearts be troubled and do not be afraid" (Jn 14:27).

Peace Is Not the Result of Power

Some people, hoping to gain a little bit more spiritually than others, have sought the power of God rather than God, the gifts of God more than God himself, and have ended up accepting Satan's counterfeits.

Satan can duplicate any of the gifts of the Spirit. There are witches' covens which specialize in healing, occult groups that speak in unknown tongues and utter accurate prophecy, and Satanists who can do what appears to be the miraculous. People who seek power for the sake of power or spiritual knowledge for its own sake can get it from Satan. By comparison with ordinary strengths it seems unusually special. But Satan can't give what mankind was designed to need, which is God himself in all of the dimensions of himself that he wants to reveal.

Although Satan can copy any of the gifts of God, he cannot duplicate the fruits of the Spirit of God. These are love, joy, peace, patience, kindness, goodness, faithfulness, gentleness and self-control (Gal 5:22) that our Lord gives to those who trust him. And what special gifts they are!

Struggle, Maybe; Presence, Yes

The peace of God, which he alone can give, cannot be artificially generated. It is not just a feeling of bliss or tranquillity—it's a fact. We may feel peaceful, but it does not mean that everything will be going smoothly.

Peace is not the absence of struggle or pain—peace comes from knowing that God is present.

When the disciples were in their boat and a storm came up, they thought Jesus was off in the hills praying—that he didn't see them. He was in the hills praying but he also saw them and came to them, calming the storm. How are things in your boat? You may not see Jesus. That doesn't mean he isn't watching you. Peace is not in quiet waters. Peace is having Jesus see you—ready to come to you.

With Jesus in your boat the anxieties caused by what is going on around will not get inside and swamp you. Rather, the anxieties themselves can become ways to peace.

The apostle Paul, reminding us of the energy-consuming drain of our anxieties said, "Do not be anxious about anything" (Phil 4:6).

At first that sounds silly. How can anyone help but be anxious? But look at it again. The apostle didn't stop there. "But in everything, by prayer and petition, with thanksgiving, present your requests to God. And the peace of God, which transcends all understanding, will guard your hearts and your minds in Christ Jesus" (Phil 4:6-7).

"Stop worrying," people say, as if just saying it will make it happen. But that's not what God is saying. His is a direct call to do something: Present your requests to God.

In other words, when anxious times come—and they will come—let them be the reminder to pray, turning the anxiety over to God, dumping it on him. That's when he will give the peace, and it will be a peace that no human being can generate, nor Satan duplicate.

You may not get clear answers when you pray. You may not need to know answers, but you will get the peace. Use the anxiety for what it is—a call to prayer, so that you can get the peace—and then live in that peace. It is deeper, wider and greater than anything we can comprehend with our ordinary understanding.

What Better Can You Have?

A Christian living in the will of God, experiencing the promise of Philippians 4:6-7, can be free and happy.

In England's Lake District, at the celebration service of the Keswick Centenary, the Reverend Harold H. Cook, at that time the oldest serving missionary in the world, stood to his feet to give his testimony. He didn't tell the assembled crowd how much he had done for Christ, nor did he reminisce about the decades he had served as a missionary. Instead, occasionally lapsing into Portuguese because of his many years in Brazil and because "I think in that language," he told of walking with Jesus and said with a resounding clear ring in his voice, "Jesus is mine; I am his; what better can you have than that?"

At ninety-seven years of age, he'd seen it all and certainly knew the struggles of living. But he had reduced the basics of life to a statement about Jesus, and as he shared it even his face said, "Peace." He had learned to do what the Bible asks us all to do: "Cast all your anxiety on him because he cares about you" (1 Pet 5:7)—and he had peace.

Can you do that—"Cast all your anxiety on him"? The answer you give tells a whole lot about where you are with God. It is a surrender, a letting go, and it doesn't just come overnight.

I came to this peace the long way around—through the back door—but I'm not sorry that I did.

I was a university student when I accepted Jesus Christ as my personal Savior and Lord. And shortly after, I felt a strong call to the ministry. It was a clear call, but I didn't want to obey it.

So I tried to dodge God, taking advantage of a business offer to shout down his call by switching my major to advertising and telling God that if he didn't want me in business, he shouldn't have offered such an attractive future.

But I was miserable.

My grades dropped, I couldn't handle the work, everything was going wrong and I knew why. Finally, in the quietness of my room, I threw down my books and said, "Okay, God, you win. If you want me in the ministry, I'll go. But whatever happens, it's all your fault!"

The misery ended, peace came, and I have never regretted that step. God has verified for me in countless ways since that this is exactly the direction he wanted me to go.

Resting Faith

Peace came out of that struggle with God. And as a result, just as I was ready to blame him for the failure that I was certain would come, I cannot claim credit for any successes that have come. The results of his owning my life have come from him, and whatever pleasure he may be deriving from all of this, it is hard to comprehend that it could be any greater than the pleasure and enjoyment that I am getting from it. When God takes hold and gives that inner peace—that sense that we are doing the right thing—it's glorious. That glory doesn't fade—it brightens with time.

Our Lord gives more than peace when we are in his will—he gives a resting faith. It is a relaxing faith, even when everything is falling apart around us. In Jesus we don't have to be victims of circumstances anymore.

That doesn't mean we will never suffer or face trials or even death—we may very well face all of that. But so what! Many a Christian has come through to wholeness only when he has battled through the worst thing that he can imagine could happen to him. Sooner or later every Christian has to do that. I'm asking and so should you: What do I fear? What is crippling me? What is holding me back from cutting loose and living with abandonment this life that Christ gives me?

Meet the Feared Enemy

Think about the thing that you fear most and then say, "Okay, what if that comes?" After a while, if we are talking it over with God, the peace of God begins to settle the issue. We have met the feared enemy, and that enemy is no longer so terrifying.

Who of us is guaranteed health or success or three meals a day or a roof over our heads or even life? Where is any of that guaranteed in Scripture? What is guaranteed are the promises given to us by our Lord. He says, "I will give you rest," and, "I go to prepare a place for you," and, "I am with you always, even unto the end of the world," and, "Take my yoke upon you . . . it's easy," and, "If you ask anything in my name I will do it." These promises come to us like blank checks waiting for us to cash whenever we want to. His checks are as certain as he is himself.

Not many of us would include the agony of a cross in our own plans for following Christ. But the cross came to him, and the servant is certainly no greater than his master. Nowhere did our Lord tell us we will definitely escape such a thing. But we are not called to contemplate it or worry about it. We are called to follow him. The disciple is a follower, a learner at the teacher's feet. He goes where his Lord directs without looking back. Peace comes not in choosing the path for ourselves, or avoiding difficulties or even praying for escape. Peace comes in being so close to him that his enveloping love surrounds us, keeping us. That's peace—even on a cross.

Get It—Keep It

He told us how to get it and how to keep it. He said, "I am the true vine and my Father is the gardener . . . . Remain in me, and I will remain in you. No branch can bear fruit by itself; it must remain in the vine. Neither can you bear fruit unless you remain in me . . . . If you remain in me and my words remain in you, ask whatever you wish, and it will be given you. This is to my Father's glory, that you bear much fruit, showing your selves to be my disciples" (Jn 15:1, 4-5, 7-8).

To abide in him is to live, but to be separated is to dry up and die. Peace is part of abiding. It is a byproduct. He calls us to that resting position in himself, not to dominate us but to live through us. The One who does not panic or fear wants to live in us. He is the same

One who is coming again. What he gives now is forever. It doesn't diminish, it increases. Isaiah knew it. He wrote, "You will keep in perfect peace him whose mind is steadfast, because he trusts in you" (Is 26:3).

Getting peace and keeping it is not luck or a gift that only some have, or something determined by fate. It centers on one truth—Jesus Christ. He is the source of peace. To have him is to have peace, and to have peace is to enjoy the daily walk that means abundant living with all the purpose and happiness that he intended us to have. Some people will miss it, and that's too bad because no one has to.

One thing is certain—you don't have to miss it. And maybe it's time now to find a quiet place alone where you can drop to your knees and tell him what he has been waiting too long already to hear: "Take me, Lord Jesus, into the center of your will."

Living in Jesus you will not only know the will of God for your life, you will have Life itself in the center of his will. There really is no other place to be.

8

A Second Look

There *is something more!*

There are basic promises of God that stand like foundation stones for our life building. These promises have been given to each of us.

Maybe these should have been presented in the beginning of this book. But some promises of God are so well known and we have heard them so often that we tend to shut them out. It is possible to overlook, even callously shrug off, the investment of God in his people. Had these promises been presented earlier some might have said, "Sure, I know that," and then ignored them.

The biblical record and church history prove that God knows his own and takes care of them. "The LORD Almighty *is* with us; the God of Jacob *is* our fortress" (Ps

46:7). "Know that the LORD is God. It is he who made us, and we are his; we *are* his people, the sheep of his pasture" (Ps 100:3). This is certain—it is settled.

When Moses led the people of Israel out of Egypt, God was right there with them, day and night. As bleak as things looked to the travelers, God had his eye on them.

Our Lord has made a covenant, as unchangeable as he is himself. He has always, without exception, kept his Word. We who live in the security of his firm and love-tendered covenant have the certain promise, "I will never fail you nor forsake you" (Heb 13:5 RSV). When God says *never*, he doesn't mean occasionally. He means never, or he wouldn't have said it.

These are not empty words—God has made a pledge. From our own experience and the experiences of other believers whom we trust, we *know* that God does not tell lies. He keeps his Word. We can say with the psalmist, "When I am afraid, I will trust in you" (Ps 56:3).

Coming to His Promises Receptively

Maybe now, having gained some insight about finding the will of God for your life, and having begun to feel as well as mentally grasp that God does want to lead you, you can come to his Word receptively. God does want to show you which way to go and he has given you his promises to build on. These promises are as inexhaustible as he is. And, you can claim what he says for yourself.

"And surely I am with you always, to the very end of the age" (Mt 28:20).

"Trust in the LORD with all your heart, and do not rely on your own insight. In all your ways acknowledge him, and he will make straight your paths" (Prov 3:5-6 RSV).

"You may ask me for anything in my name, and I will do it" (Jn 14:14).

"Whoever comes to me I will never drive away" (Jn 6:37).

"Then you will know the truth, and the truth will set you free" (Jn 8:32).

"His divine power has given us everything we need for life and godliness through our knowledge of him who called us by his own glory and goodness" (2 Pet 1:3).

Don't stop with these—get your own Bible and keep going thoughtfully and prayerfully. You will find that God is very much involved with people. Best of all, he is involved with you.

Directions for Tomorrow

Sometimes even Christians argue: "But if I could only see into the future, that's all I ask. If I could only know for sure, then I would act with no inner reservations."

But saying that is demanding that God cater to our own lack of trust. We cannot have concrete assurance about ourselves ahead of time for the simple reason that we do not have the mind that can understand ahead of time the circumstances in which those assurances will be carried out.

If I ask for direction about tomorrow that I can know with certainty today, I am asking for directions that won't make sense to me. I won't know tomorrow until tomorrow. I don't know what that day will be—so how will I be able to understand my role in it?

Even if I could understand tomorrow and the next

day and the days after that, and see how my life's direction fits into them, I would be so overwhelmed that I probably wouldn't be able to handle it or act at all. If any of us had known ahead of time some of the mountains we have already had to scale, we would have given up. But we didn't know. Mercifully God didn't tell us. He just prepared us, without our knowing that he was preparing us, and equipped us with skills and his own promise to enter those experiences with us. Then, later, we found that by following him step by step in the leading that he gave, the mountains were conquered.

God doesn't want you to be a monument to his impotence. There is no way that anyone reading the Bible, or listening to other Christians, or recalling God's faithfulness in his own life, can come to that conclusion.

Unless—we refuse to let him act. And that's exactly what some people do, even Christians.

How many people have you met who fell in love with love, or fell in love with marriage as a dream and made their own choice about the person they married? And how many are struggling now?

How many are violating one or more of the commandments in order to satisfy themselves with the "gospel" of happiness that is touted as "what God wants for me because I am his child"?

How many scars are on your own soul from acting because God was too slow for you, knowing now that had you trusted and waited, the answer would have been there at a time when you were prepared for it?

Will you let him have his way in your life now? That's really what it all comes down to. That's the only question to be answered, and every person has to answer it—

every day. At each turn of the road that question comes and has to be answered again. Regardless of what we have done or haven't done before, will we trust him now? Will we let him be God? Will we commit ourselves to him through Jesus Christ who assured us, "I am the way and the truth and the life. No one comes to the Father except through me" (Jn 14:6)?

Will we live and act by faith? We can lead a person into a darkened room and say to him, "Flip that switch on the wall, and the lights will go on."

But if he insists that we first prove to him that the lights will go on before he risks touching the switch, we can't do it. We can tell him that the light switch has always worked. We can describe how bright the room will be; we can plead, but he has to throw the switch before he will really know. And, when he finally does it, we no longer have to explain anything—he knows.

The same is true in finding the will of God. His promises to us about his will and leading are clear. Acting on his promises is the only battle we have to fight. Once we act, we will know.

God can lead specifically, even forcefully—or he may lead very quietly. But even if we miss some clear direction, nothing stops. He is still God and can pick us up where we are and keep on leading—and he will. Even if we start late in life, he can "repay you for the years the locusts have eaten" (see Joel 2:25). He is forgiving and healing because he is loving.

There is no package that we can find labeled "God's will" with our individual names on it. It isn't like a blueprint with all the steps A through Z clearly marked, even though God knows A through Z.

We Will Understand

He is God. We are not. We don't have his understanding, his infinite wisdom or anything else that makes him omnipotent. But in the end, when the many strings are gathered together, we will see the reasons for the loving careful leading he has been giving us all life long—and we will understand.

When someone realizes—maybe after years of spiritual blindness—that God has been reaching out to him, and then responds, he moves into a new relationship with God. He did not love first, God did. He did not initiate the cross, God did. And at last, overwhelmed by the love of God that kept on coming—all the way to Calvary and past it—he turns back to that cross to learn what he could never understand before: "You are not your own; you were bought at a price" (1 Cor 6:19-20).

Those who are obedient are no longer their own. Having been bought with a price and paid for, they are servants, sons and daughters. They do not spend all of their time in debate about the meaning of their position or asking questions about it; they live it.

That obedience may result in a comfortable life, simply because life is comfortable around us. It may result in a horrible existence, because life is a horror around us. But it will result in Life, life with a capital L that only God can give. It is a life that never ends.

In Christ we have more than just the fullest life or the happiest life, or even the most satisfying life. These are relative statements—we live in the context of Philippians 4:11-12 (RSV), "Not that I complain of want; for I have learned, in whatever state I am, to be content. I know how to be abased, and I know how to abound; in any and all circumstances I have learned the secret of facing plenty and hunger, abundance and want."

But Always We Have Life

As believers, the only life we have is placed in the hands of the One who asks us, in the words of St. Paul, to present our bodies "as living sacrifices, holy and pleasing to God—which is your spiritual worship" (Rom 12:1). And when we do that we are able to shout with Paul, "I can do all things in him who strengthens me" (Phil 4:13).

To the extent that we are capable of knowing anything about the divine mind of God, we are able to know his will for our lives. Any more than what he reveals we cannot know. But if we will walk in the light of what he has revealed and be responsive and not kick against his leading or argue with him, then we won't have to wonder about our tomorrows anymore.

We won't always be trying to peek around life's corners. We can live, relaxed in the confidence that God guides our tomorrows.

And, content in that certainty, we can reach out and take hold of a beautiful promise: "No eye has seen, nor ear heard, nor the heart of man conceived what God has prepared for those who love him" (1 Cor 2:9).

With the childlikeness that Jesus asked for in his followers, we can look at the wonders around us and, ready for his best, ask with a smile on our faces and happiness in our hearts—and a bit of a tremble from the excitement of anticipation—"Which way, Lord?"